Johannes Brahms

Symphony No. 3 in F major / F-Dur

Op. 90

Edited by / Herausgegeben von
Richard Clarke

EULENBURG

EAS 119
ISBN 978-3-7957-6519-4
ISMN M-2002-2342-2

Contents / Inhalt

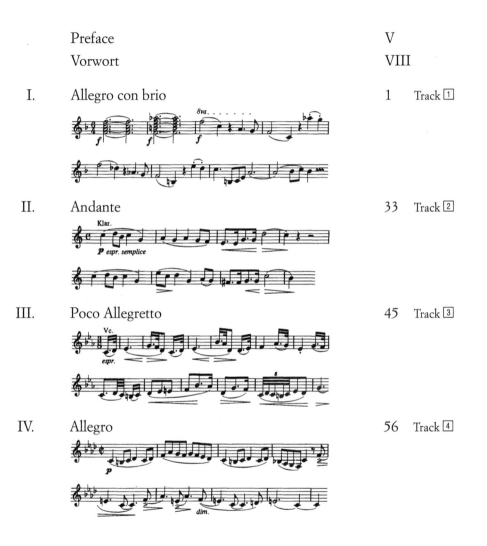

Preface

Composed: 1883 in Wiesbaden (completed)
First performance: 2 December 1883 in Vienna, conducted by Hans Richter
Original publisher: Simrock, Berlin, March 1884
Instrumentation: 2 Flutes, 2 Oboes, 2 Clarinets, 2 Bassoons,
Contrabassoon – 4 Horns, 2 Trumpets, 3 Trombones – Timpani – Strings
Duration: ca. 33 minutes

With the exception of a single authenticated fact, the genesis of Brahms's Third Symphony is beset by speculation. All that we can say for certain is that the composer completed work on the score during the summer of 1883, when he was staying in rooms at 19 Geisenbergstraße, Wiesbaden, rooms that he described to his friend Theodor Billroth in a letter postmarked 27 June 1883: 'I'm leading a charmed life here, almost as if I were trying to emulate Wagner! The place was originally built as a studio but was later turned into the most delightful of country houses, and a studio like this one provides a wonderfully high, cool and airy room!' Brahms generally destroyed all material relating to the compositional process and said little or nothing to his friends about his current work on a piece, so that the absence of any surviving sources makes it impossible to say if he composed the whole of his Third Symphony in this studio in Wiesbaden or if he merely wrote out the full score on the basis of existing drafts and preliminary sketches. This statement may surprise readers familiar with the claims advanced by Brahms's first biographer, Max Kalbeck, who in the third volume of his biography argues on the strength of a letter that the composer wrote to his publisher, Fritz Simrock, on 15 September 1883 that 'the first movement already existed at an earlier period, albeit in a different form'. But the letter to Simrock nowhere refers to the Third Symphony in so many words. Rather, the passage in question appears to relate to the String Quintet op. 88, a point made many years ago by Hans Gál: its slow movement is based on a sarabande for piano that Brahms had first noted down in February 1855. By the same token, Kalbeck's claim that 'the two inner movements [of the Third Symphony] are only loosely connected to the rest of the work and owe their existence to the composer's preoccupation with Goethe's *Faust*' is pure speculation. (Kalbeck is referring here to the incidental music for a production of *Faust* that the director of the Vienna Burgtheater, Franz Dingelstedt, invited Brahms to write in 1880.) But no such incidental music has survived, rendering any speculations about it otiose, quite apart from which the claim that the inner movements are only loosely related to the rest of the symphony is simply not tenable, so close are the links between these two movements and the others. Finally, Kalbeck's comments on the final Allegro ('evidently the last movement to be written inasmuch as it had no place in the work's original plan') reveal his imagination working overtime: its genesis and intellectual ideas, he argues, were closely bound up with the composer's visit to the Niederwald to see the statue of Germania that commemorated the Franco-Prussian War of 1870–71 and the resultant foundation of Bismarck's Reich. Six years in the making, this monument was officially inaugurated on 28 September 1883.

The conductor Franz Wüllner was the first to be told about the existence of the Third Symphony. Next came Clara Schumann and Joseph Joachim. Only then did Brahms inform his publisher Fritz Simrock and entrust the score to him. (A version for piano four hands appeared in March/April 1884, followed by the full score and performing parts in May 1884.) The work received its first performance in Vienna on 2 December 1883 under the direction of Hans Richter. According to Kalbeck, 'troops from the Wagner–Bruckner *ecclesia militans* were positioned in the standing area of the Musikvereinssaal' and hissed the performance, but in spite of this, the work was a triumphant success: 'The composer was tumultuously acclaimed and repeatedly called out on to the platform after the first, third and final movements,' wrote the reviewer of the *Signale für die musikalische Welt*, while the Viennese music critic Eduard Hanslick felt that 'on an outward level, too, the success of the new symphony at the Philharmonic concert was one of the most brilliant'.

Reviewers judged the new symphony by the standards set its two predecessors, the First Symphony in C minor op. 68 and the Second Symphony in D major op. 73, noting that in every case the composer had remained true to traditional four-movement form, while typically turning away from the sort of Adagio and Scherzo that Beethoven had retained in his symphonies. They also observed that the techniques of thematic development and developing variation that Brahms had used in his First and Second Symphonies in order to solve the problem of large-scale form also played a decisive role in his Third. They further felt that the melodic, rhythmic, harmonic and technical subtleties with which Brahms had experimented in his first two symphonies and which, with their added sense of piquancy, are so characteristic of his musical language in general are also found in his Third Symphony. In short, his progress as a symphonist was a seamless and organic continuation of the journey on which he had set out in his earlier contributions to the medium. Among the novel elements that set the Third Symphony apart from its two predecessors was felt to be the opening of the work, its three-bar 'motto' theme functioning as a leitmotif that permeates the formal musical argument of the whole of the opening movement. Another striking feature was the brevity of the development sections of the two outer movements, a brevity that gives the impression that Brahms was consciously avoiding any sense of opposition between their themes in favour of their harmonious coexistence. Also emphasized was Brahms's interest in cyclical form, an interest that finds far more compelling expression in the Third Symphony than in either the First or the Second. The theme heard in the transition of the final movement harks back to the second theme of the Andante; the second subject of the finale reveals similarities to the main theme of the third movement; and at the end of the final Allegro Brahms introduces an almost literal quotation of the final bars of the opening movement, thereby forging a cyclical link with the beginning of the work and turning the symphony's four movements into a fully integrated symphonic whole. But the most salient feature of the Third Symphony remains the eloquence of its musical language: note in particular the curious way in which the opening and closing movements both fade gently away; note, too, the use of chorale harmonies, the folk-like element and the work's lyrical inwardness. Max Kalbeck was the first to comment on this aspect of the piece in his biography of the composer: 'No one who has taken a detailed interest in the F major Symphony has been able to resist the temptation to impute to it a particular poetic content or programme.' 'What poetry!' wrote Clara Schumann; 'How one feels enveloped from first to last by the mysterious magic of life in the forest!' And, writing to the composer, Joseph Joachim had the following to say about the final movement: 'It's curious but, however little time I generally have for trivialising interpretations that seek out poetry in music, I cannot rid my mind of a particular poetical image in this work: Hero and Leander.' And on 10 October 1884, Antonín Dvořák, who was a close friend of Brahms and who knew parts of the Third Symphony from a performance to which the composer had treated him on the piano in Vienna, wrote to Fritz Simrock: 'I am not exaggerating when I say that this work surpasses both his earlier symphonies, if not perhaps in greatness and the power of its conception, then certainly in terms of its beauty! It contains a mood not often found in Brahms! What glorious melodies there are here! It is love pure and simple, and on hearing it your heart overflows. Remember what I have said, and when you hear the symphony, you will say that I heard aright.'

Klaus Döge
Translation: Stewart Spencer

Vorwort

komponiert: 1883 in Wiesbaden (Kompositionsabschluss)
Uraufführung: 2. Dezember 1883 in Wien unter der Leitung
von Hans Richter
Originalverlag: N. Simrock, Berlin, März 1884
Orchesterbesetzung: 2 Flöten, 2 Oboen, 2 Klarinetten, 2 Fagotte,
Kontrafagott – 4 Hörner, 2 Trompeten, 3 Posaunen – Pauken – Streicher
Spieldauer: etwa 33 Minuten

Hinsichtlich der Entstehungsgeschichte der dritten Sinfonie von Johannes Brahms ist nur ein zuverlässiges Faktum bekannt: der Kompositionsabschluss im Sommer 1883. Brahms verbrachte seine damaligen Sommerferien in Wiesbaden, untergebracht in einer Wohnung in der Geisenbergstraße Nr. 19 und in einem Haus, das der Komponist seinem Freund Theodor Billroth gegenüber mit den Worten beschrieb: „Ich wohne hier reizend, aber als ob ich es Wagner nachtun wollte! Ursprünglich [...] als Atelier gebaut, ist es nachträglich zum hübschesten Landhaus geworden, und so ein Atelier gibt ein herrliches hohes, kühles, lustiges Zimmer!" Die Frage, ob Brahms in diesem Zimmer damals seine dritte Sinfonie als Ganzes neu komponierte oder sie an Hand bereits existierender Entwürfe und Vorskizzierungen in Partitur ausarbeitete, muss – wie so oft bei diesem Komponisten, der zumeist alle Materialien seines Arbeitsprozesses vernichtete und seine aktuelle kompositorische Arbeit nur spärlich oder gar nicht Freunden gegenüber andeutete – fehlender Quellen wegen offen bleiben. Diese Aussage mag überraschen angesichts der Angaben des ersten Brahms-Biografen Max Kalbeck. Im dritten Band seiner Brahmsbiografie schreibt er, sich auf einen Brief des Komponisten an den Verleger Simrock vom 15. September 1883 stützend, dass „der erste Satz in anderer Form schon in früher Zeit existierte." Doch wird in dem besagten Brief die dritte Sinfonie von Brahms an keiner Stelle expressis verbis erwähnt oder auf sie verwiesen; die Briefstelle scheint vielmehr – wie Hans Gál zeigte – auf das Streichquintett op. 88 gemünzt gewesen zu sein, in dessen langsamen Satz eine Klaviersarabande kompositorisch Verwendung fand, die Brahms bereits im Februar 1855 niedergeschrieben hatte. Auch Kalbecks Ausführung, „daß die Mittelsätze [der 3. Sinfonie], die als ein mit dem Übrigen nur lose verknüpftes Ganze für sich zu betrachten sind, der Beschäftigung mit Goethes *Faust* ihr Dasein verdanken", – eine Ausführung, die Bezug nimmt auf eine Bühnenmusik zu Goethes *Faust*, zu der Brahms 1880 vom Leiter des Wiener Burgtheaters Franz Dingelstedt angeregt wurde –, bleibt spekulativ: Zum einen, weil man die Bühnenmusik als solche gar nicht kennt; und zum anderen, weil der Befund, die Mittelsätze seien mit dem Rest der Sinfonie nur lose verknüpft, angesichts der motivisch-thematischen Verbindungen zwischen den Mittelsätzen und dem Kopf- und Finalsatz analytisch gesehen nicht haltbar ist. Und literarisch überschäumende Fantasie schließlich stellen Kalbecks Ausführungen zum Finale („offenbar das jüngste Stück der Symphonie, [das] im ursprünglichen Plan des Werkes keine Stelle hatte") dar, dessen Entstehung und geistigen Inhalt er mit Brahms' nachweislichem Besuch der an den Krieg von 1870/71 und die damit zusammenhängende deutsche Reichsgründung erinnernden Germania-Figur im Niederwald-Denkmal, welches nach sechsjähriger Bauzeit am 28. September 1883 feierlich eröffnet wurde, in engsten Zusammenhang brachte.

Die 3. Sinfonie, von deren Existenz Brahms als erstem dem Dirigenten Franz Wüllner, dann auch Clara Schumann und Joseph Joachim Bescheid gab, bevor er sie seinem Verleger Fritz Simrock zur Publikation überließ (der vierhändige Klavierauszug erschien im März/April 1884, die Partitur und Stimmen wurden im Mai 1884 publiziert), erlebte ihre Uraufführung am 2. Dezember 1883 in Wien unter der Leitung von Hans Richter. Der Erfolg, den die Sinfonie dabei erzielte, war – trotz des Zischens einer „im Stehparterre des Musikvereinssaales postierten Truppe der Wagner-Brucknerschen ecclesia militans" – ein für Brahms triumphaler: „Nach dem ersten, dritten und dem Schlußsatze wurde der Componist stürmisch und wiederholt gerufen.", hieß es im Premierenbericht der *Signale für die musikalische Welt*, und der Wiener Musikkritiker Eduard Hanslick schrieb in seiner Aufführungskritik: „Der Erfolg der neuen Symphonie im Philharmonischen Concerte gehörte auch äußerlich zu den glänzendsten."

In den Werkrezensionen selbst wurde dabei das neue symphonische Werk an Brahms' vorausgegangenen Sinfonien, der Sinfonie Nr. 1 c-Moll, op. 68, und der Sinfonie Nr. 2 D-Dur, op. 73, gemessen und festgestellt, dass Brahms hier wie dort an der traditionellen Viersätzigkeit mit der für ihn typischen Abkehr vom Adagio- und Scherzotypus Beethovenscher Symphonik festhielt; dass auch in seiner Dritten die zuvor in der ersten und zweiten Sinfonie erprobten Techniken der Themenverarbeitung und entwickelnden Variation zur Bewältigung der großen Form eine entscheidende Rolle spielten; und dass auch in die dritte Sinfonie jene für Brahms musikalische Sprache insgesamt so charakteristischen melodischen, rhythmischen, harmonischen und satztechnischen Pikanterien aufwies; dass also – summa summarum – Brahms' Weg als Symphoniker sich in der Dritten nahtlos und organisch an das vorangegangene Schaffen anschloss. Als neu und anders gegenüber den ersten beiden Sinfonien empfunden wurde zum einen der Werkbeginn mit seinem dreitaktigen musikalischen Motto, das wie ein roter Faden den formalen Verlauf des ersten Satz durchzieht. Als auffällig angesehen wurde zum anderen die Kürze der Durchführungsteile der beiden Ecksätze, die den Eindruck erweckt, als wolle Brahms hier dem Gegeneinander der Themen zugunsten eines thematischen Miteinanders bewusst aus dem Weg gehen. Als besonderes hervorgehoben wurde des weiteren Brahms' Bemühen um den zyklischen Zusammenhang, – ein Bemühen, das in der Dritten wie in keiner der beiden vorausgegangenen Sinfonien sich bemerkbar macht: Das Überleitungsthema im Schlusssatz entspricht dem Kontrastgedanken des zweiten Satzes, das Seitenthema des Finales weist Ähnlichkeiten zum Hauptthema des dritten Satzes auf und am Ende des Finales zitiert Brahms die Schlusstakte des Kopfsatzes fast tongetreu, dadurch kompositorisch eine zyklische Brücke zum Anfang der Sinfonie schaffend, unter der sich alle vier Sätze zum symphonischen Ganzen seiner dritten Sinfonie vereinen. Als hervorstechendste Eigenart aber galt (und gilt bis heute) das Sprechende der Musik in Brahms' dritter Sinfonie mit ihrem eigenartig ruhigen Ausklingen des Kopf- und

Finalsatzes, mit ihrer Choralidiomatik, ihrem Volksliedhaften und ihrer lyrischen Verinnerlichung: Schon Max Kalbeck hatte in seiner Brahms-Biografie geschrieben: „Wer immer sich eingehender mit der F-dur-Symphonie beschäftigte, hat der Versuchung, ihr einen besonderen poetischen Inhalt, ein Programm, unterzulegen, nicht ausweichen können." „Welche Poesie, [...] Wie ist man von Anfang bis zu Ende umfangen von dem geheimnisvollen Zauber des Waldlebens" äußerte Clara Schumann; in Zusammenhang mit dem Finalsatz schrieb Joseph Joachim an Brahms: „Und sonderbar, so wenig ich das Deuteln auf Poesie in der Musik in der Regel liebe, werde ich doch bei dem Stück [...] ein bestimmtes poetisches Bild nicht los: Hero und Leander!"; und am 10. Oktober 1884 richtete der mit Brahms eng befreundete Prager Komponist Antonín Dvořák, dem Brahms in Wien damals Teile seines Opus 90 am Klavier vorgespielt hatte, an den Verleger Fritz Simrock die Worte: „Ich sage und übertreibe nicht, daß dieses Werk seine beiden ersten Sinfonien überragt; wenn auch nicht vielleicht an Größe und mächtiger Konzeption – so aber gewiß an – Schönheit! Es ist eine Stimmung drin, wie man sie bei Brahms nicht oft findet! Welch herrliche Melodien sind da zu finden! Es ist lauter Liebe und das Herz geht einem dabei auf. Denken Sie an meine Worte und wenn Sie die Sinfonie hören, werden Sie sagen, daß ich gut gehört habe."

Klaus Döge

Symphony No. 3

Johannes Brahms
(1833–1897)
Op. 90

I. Allegro con brio

EAS 119

© 2007 Ernst Eulenburg Ltd, London
and Ernst Eulenburg & Co GmbH, Mainz

A

9

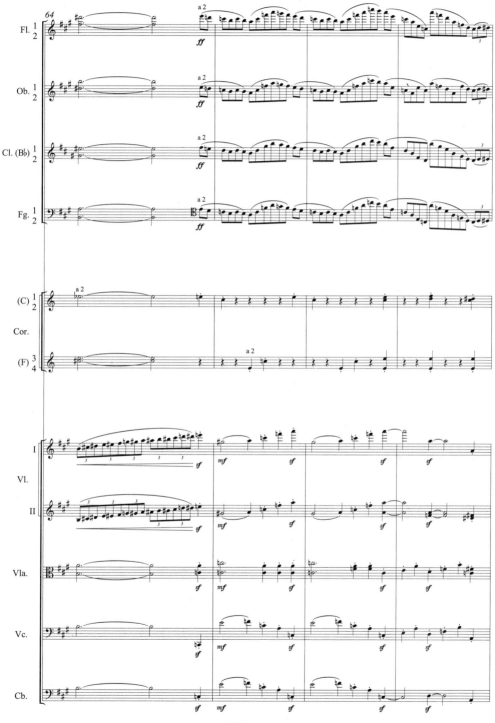

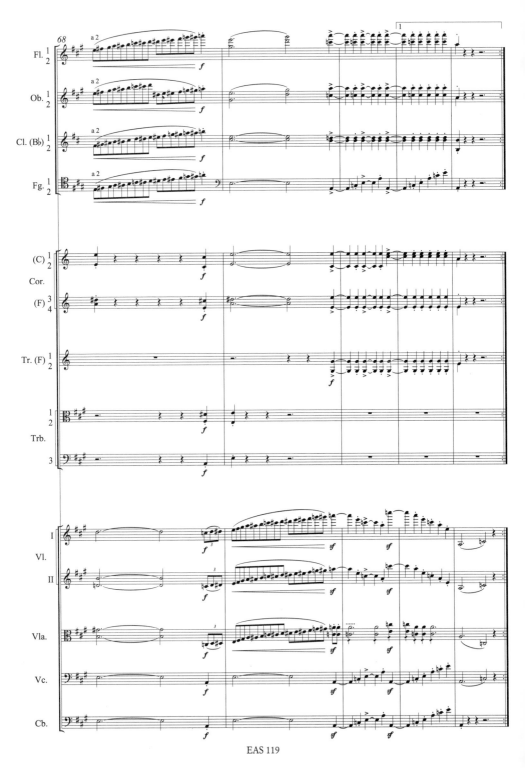

14

G

Tempo I

20

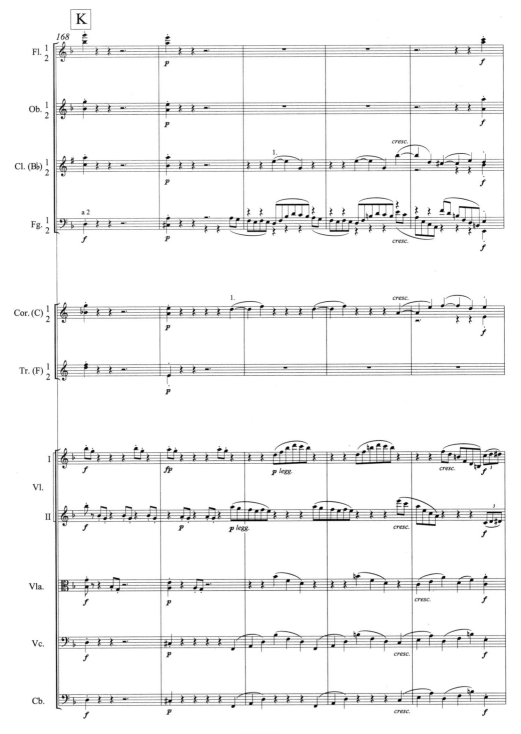

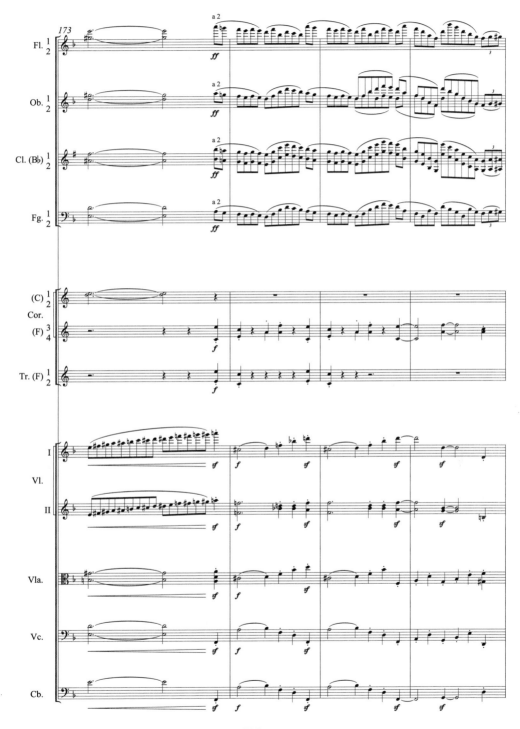

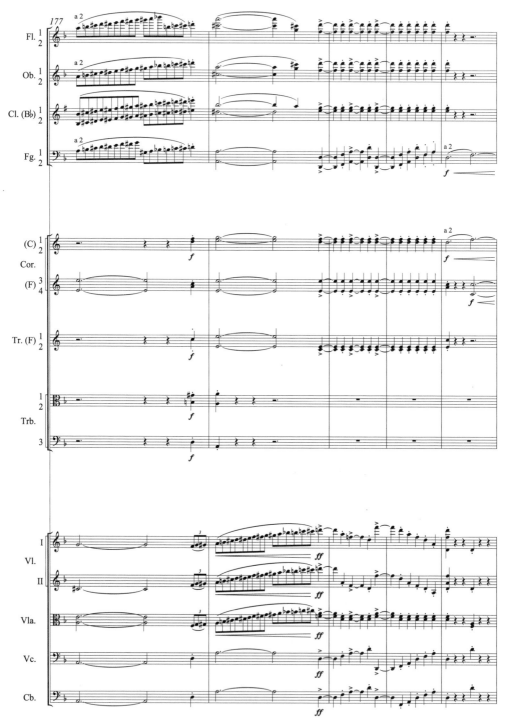

II. Andante

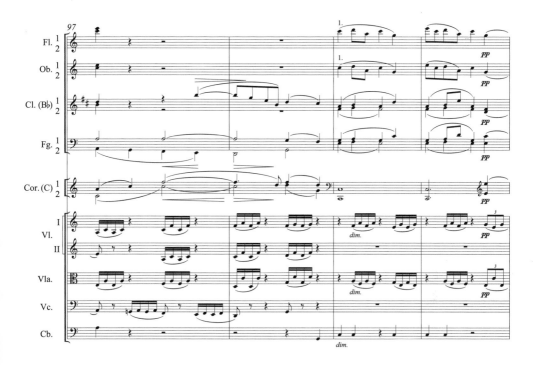

44

III. Poco Allegretto

A

IV. Allegro

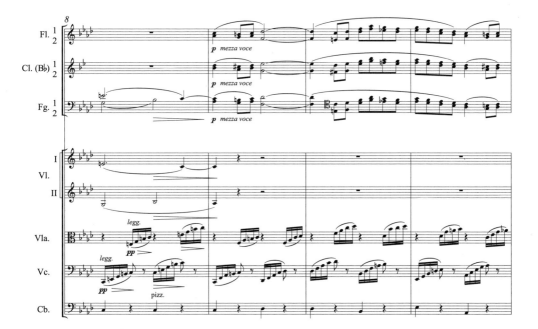

60

62

EAS 119

74

M

86

Un poco sostenuto

Printed in China